# How To Keep Safe

...in a sometimes scary world

## Jo FitzGerald

Illustrated by Ros Webb

Published by Tiny Sponges Ltd.
1 Grove Road, Worthing BN14 9DQ, UK
http://www.tinysponges.com/keeping-safe

ISBN PAPERBACK: 978-1-9999379-0-4

Printed in UK

# Introduction

All parents want to keep their children safe – physically safe, and mentally and emotionally strong. The world we live in can be a very worrying and sometimes scary place, and we're not always in control of what may come our way – or what our children are exposed to.

This book covers some of those situations we worry about most and provides a simple, positive and constructive way of talking about topics we may often avoid. Because we don't want to worry or scare our children do we? We want to protect them...

I'm a parent, a grandparent, a teacher – so I understand all of that. I too have experienced scary situations. What is proven to help deal with worry and anxiety – for you as an adult and for your child – it's to **have a plan**, to **know what to do**. It arms you, it empowers you, it reassures you. It's being responsible – and knowing how to respond. That's it! Easy!

Enjoy the book together – I mean that: **enjoy** it. It's not a scary story, it's a story about kind people who help us, and about how **we** can be strong, happy and safe.


Jo FitzGerald

For Emma. May you always be safe and strong and have a plan.

There are people around who help us,
  if we're hurt or in harm's way.
Like nurses or like doctors,
  the police, the fire brigade.

But they can't be with us everywhere,
like the park or the museum.
Or at your school, or on holiday;
we very rarely see them.

So, you need to know a thing or… three
  about keeping safe and sound.
Just in case things DO go wrong
  – in case help just can't be found.

At school, you practise what to do
if the fire alarm goes off.
But you need more plans for emergencies;
not just fires, but other stuff.
"What happens if I'm in a crowd
And I lose my mum or dad."
Or if someone's hurt, or if someone's near,
that you think just might be bad?

'Cos not everyone around is nice;
    some people do us harm.
The first thing that you need to do
    is sound out an alarm.
Find a trusted adult near you.
It's quite alright to say:
"This guy's a little crazy,
    and I just don't feel OK."

Because sometimes there are people
    who try to hurt us bad.
They're human, but they're nasty,
    and often they are sad.
But when they try to do something
    to hurt somebody else,
You need to know what you can do
    so, you're not hurt yourself.

If something happens, think about
    the things that you could do.
Do you need to run?
Do you need to hide?
What's the safest thing for **you**?

Maybe you are somewhere
that you've never been before.
Think to yourself: "If things go wrong,
then where's the nearest door?"
The best doors say EMERGENCY,
with EXIT underneath
This means a way to get outside,
a safe way to the street.

So, if things are turning crazy
and someone's going wild,
can you safely run away from them?
Or best be quiet and hide?

EMERGENCY
EXIT

PUSH

If you see some smoke or fire
   and you think it's kind of near,
It's OK to be worried
   and it's OK to feel fear.

Is there a FIRE ALARM that you can push
   to send out a warning sound?
If there is smoke up in the air,
   then stay close to the ground.

FIRE
PLAN
1. SHOUT
2. GET DOWN
3. GET OUT

If you're alone, can you shout for help?
Can you crawl your way outside?
Does your family have a fire plan?
Remember NOT to hide.

If you're walking round the market
   or maybe in a crowd.
And you realise that Mum or Dad
   are no longer around...
What's the best way you can find them?
Do you have a meet-up spot?
Somewhere to go if things go wrong?
Don't worry if there's not.

Can you find someone who works there?
(With a name badge on their chest.)
Just tell them that you think you're lost
– and they will do the rest.
They'll ask your name, ask who you're with.
They'll make you feel OK.
And mum and dad will hear you're found
and soon be on their way.

So, whether you are in or out,
  PLAN and be prepared
  for keeping safe and keeping strong.
You'll find you're not so scared.

Sometimes you may hear the news
    on the radio or the telly.
Or even from your mum or dad
    – or Great Big Auntie Nelly.

That something bad has happened,
    something ever so not nice.
And you see people are angry
    or you may see people cry.

And you have a lot of questions!
    Well, go on – just ask about.
We'll try to help you understand
    and figure it all out.

WHY?

HOW

WHO?

WHAT'S HAPPENED?

?

?

?

?

?

And lastly – it's important,
    I feel I need to say...
That as you go about your life,
    as you do things day by day:
    you won't really need to worry.
Because things WILL be alright!
The sun will shine, you'll play, you'll laugh.
You'll have lovely dreams at night.

But – just in case, you'll be prepared.
You'll know what you can do.
Be proud of that: feel safe, feel loved.
Live life! – you perfect **you**.

# Things to Talk About – Parents, Caregivers and Educators

One of the most important things we can do for our children is keep them safe; not just physically – but mentally safe, in a good place. There are all kinds of things going on in the world that are scary, both for us as adults and for our children. We may think that we shield our children from most of this, and I'm sure we do – but to what extent?

Do you know? Are you sure? How can we monitor what is said to our children at school, in the playground? What if they hear about frightening events on the radio or TV? Or overhear adults talking, or see a reaction to news? Perhaps not even at home, but when they are with friends, at their houses, in their cars... Sometimes we underestimate what children absorb, and sometimes we avoid those difficult conversations – because we don't want to worry or scare them. We want to protect them.

But if we talk about our worries, if we share them, if we HAVE A PLAN and everyone KNOWS WHAT TO DO, well, it makes us stronger. It gives us power and it reassures and eases that worry and anxiety for adult and child.

I hope this book helps you do just that with your child. It's important to be able to talk about scary things, things that worry us, things that we don't understand – to ask questions, to figure things out. Avoidance or denial can just feed the worry, grow the anxiety – until it becomes this BIG SCARY THING! Let's not go there; let's talk – and plan – together. And you know what? Chances are it'll never happen... NEVER.

Use this part of the book to help you ask and answer any questions that may come up. It will help you teach how it's important to talk about our feelings and to know what to do.

If you have any comments or suggestions for improving this book, we'd love to hear from you. Just send us an email at info@tinysponges.com.

# Things To Talk About

## Pages 2 & 3

Can you think of anyone else who helps us? How do these people help us? What kind of people do you think they are? Kind? Caring? Helpful? Brave? When might we need these people to help us? How do these people make you feel?

## Pages 4 & 5

What is a plan? What does practising mean? Why is it good to practise things?

## Pages 6 & 7

How might you know that someone wants to hurt you? Would it be a good idea to tell someone you know, if you are worried? Why is it important to move away from people who are worrying you? What do you think worrying behaviour looks like?

Why might it be good to hide? Why should we be really quiet if we hide? Why might it be good to run? How could we escape from somewhere? Where would we go to that would be safe? Who could we tell? How could we make a plan? What should be in our plan?

## Pages 8 & 9

How would you know there was a bad fire nearby? What would you shout to get help? What number should you dial on a phone? What would you say to the operator? What does a fire alarm look like? Where is the smoke alarm at home? What does it sound like?

Why should we stay close to the ground if there is smoke? Why should we practice getting out of the home? Why is it a good idea to practice crawling out of your home? Why should you never hide if there is a fire?

## Pages 10 & 11

Why is it important to stay close to the adult that you're with? Why should you shout out loudly if you can't see your adult? Why should you stay still and not run? Why is it important to have a plan of what to do if you get lost somewhere? How would you know who to tell that you're lost? What would you tell them?

# Things To Talk About

## Pages 12 & 13

Is there anything for which you would like to make a plan? Which number do we call in an emergency? What is an emergency?

## Pages 14 & 15

Do you think it is a good think to talk to someone about your worries? Why is it a good idea to ask questions?

## Pages 16 & 17

What makes you feel safe? What makes you feel happy?

For a more detailed FREE information pack go to:

www.howtokeepsafe.info/infopack

The pack contains

- tips and detailed safety advice for you and your children
- safety plan templates
- links to useful websites
- links to recommended safety equipment and aids.

# NOTES

You can use this page to list your plans, write down what's been agreed, or anything else that can help you KEEP SAFE...

# NOTES

You can use this page to list your plans, write down what's been agreed, or anything else that can help you KEEP SAFE...